Rugby Union

Produced in collaboration with
the Rugby Football Union

RUGBY FOOTBALL UNION

Produced for A & C Black by

Monkey Puzzle Media Ltd
Gissings Farm, Fressingfield
Suffolk IP21 5SH

Published in 2006 by

A & C Black Publishers Ltd
38 Soho Square, London W1D 3HB
www.acblack.com

Sixth edition 2006

Note: While every effort has been made to ensure
that the content of this book is as technically accurate
and as sound as possible, neither the author nor the
publisher can accept responsibility for any injury or
loss sustained as a result of the use of this material.

A & C Black uses paper produced with elemental
chlorine-free pulp, harvested from managed
sustainable forests.

Acknowledgements
Cover and inside design by James Winrow for
Monkey Puzzle Media Ltd
The publishers would like to thank Gilbert for their
photographic contribution to this book (pages 7 and 9).
Front cover photograph courtesy of Getty Images.
Photograph on page 12 courtesy of Action Plus Sports
Images. Phtographs on pages 45, 46, 47, 48, 49, 51
and 52 courtesy of Gareth Jones/Sports-alive.com.
All other photographs courtesy of Empics.
Illustrations by Daniel Rogers (page 10) and Ron Dixon
at TechType

KNOW THE GAME is a registered trademark.

Printed and bound in China by C&C Offset Printing Co., Ltd

Note: Throughout the book players and officials are
referred to as 'he'. This should, of course, be taken to
mean 'he or she' where appropriate.

CONTENTS

THE GAME

Rugby union is played by two teams of 15 players, normally on grass – it is possible to play on other surfaces, such as sand, as long as these do not make the game dangerous. The object of rugby union is to score tries and kick goals. Tries are scored when a player grounds the ball in the in-goal area at the opposition's end of the pitch. Goals are scored by kicking the ball between the opponents' goalposts, above the crossbar.

THE LAWS

The laws of rugby union are framed and interpreted by the International Rugby Board (IRB). They apply to nearly all matches played in the countries represented on the Board (which is most rugby-playing countries). The main part of this book explains the adult version of rugby. Variations for different age groups are on pages 40–53.

THE PITCH

The diagram below shows the markings and maximum dimensions of the playing area. All pitches should be as near as possible to the maximum dimensions shown. The field of play is inside the inner edge of its boundary lines, and does not include the goal lines, touchlines, or the in-goal area in which tries are scored.

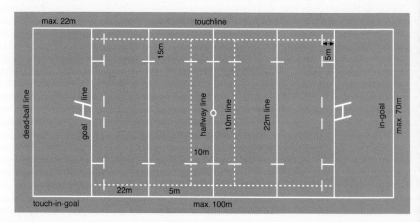

Marking lines should be clearly defined and all the same width, made with whiting or chalk and not more than 10cm wide. Ruts should not be cut in the turf.

THE GOAL

The goal stands in the centre of the goal line. It is made of two upright posts, 5.6m apart, joined by a crossbar 3m off the ground.

> **The goalposts are judged to extend indefinitely upwards – a kicker still scores if their kick is on target, but higher than the tops of the posts.**

FLAGPOSTS

Flagposts are placed to mark:

- corners of the goal lines and touchlines

- the 22m and halfway lines (these are normally placed about 1m outside the touchline)

- the corners of the dead-ball lines and the touch-in-goal lines.

The posts should be upright and a minimum of 1.2m high, but not too firmly fixed, so that they will give way if a player falls against them.

Tries are scored by grounding the ball in the opposition's in-goal area. Here, the England wing Mark Cueto is about to ground the ball.

THE BALL

Rugby is played with an oval four-panelled ball. The outer casing encloses an air-inflated bladder. Nothing should be used in the construction that could injure the players. The lacing, if there is any, should be given careful consideration so that the outer casing is neatly closed.

PLAYERS

The names of the positions occupied by the players, and the numbers worn by them, are governed by IRB regulations. The graphic below shows their positions and names.

FULL–SIZE BALL

A rugby ball must have the following dimensions:

- weight: 400–440g
- length in line: 280–300mm
- circumference (end on): 760–790mm
- circumference (in width): 580–620mm.

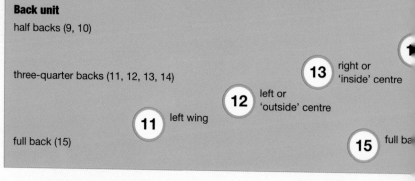

Forward unit

front row forwards (1, 2, 3)

second row forwards (4, 5)

back row forwards (6, 7, 8)

1 loose-head prop

6 blind-side flanker

4

lock

Back unit

half backs (9, 10)

three-quarter backs (11, 12, 13, 14)

13 right or 'inside' centre

12 left or 'outside' centre

11 left wing

full back (15)

15 full back

The official ball of England Rugby.

REPLACEMENTS

- Up to two substitutes of front-row players and up to five substitutes of other players may be made for any other reason.

- A player with a blood injury must leave the pitch until the bleeding has been stopped. Another player comes on as a temporary replacement.

- Other injured players are replaced permanently and must not resume playing unless they are needed to replace a player with a bleeding wound, or for an injured front-row player (if there is no alternative).

- If a front-row forward is ordered off and no other player on the field can play in the front row, the captain may nominate another player to leave the field and be replaced by a substitute front-row forward.

- If, because of sending off or injury, a team cannot provide enough suitable trained front-row players, the match continues with uncontested scrums.

hooker **3** tight-head prop

5 lock **7** open-side flanker

number eight

9 scrum half

alf (or 'outside or 'standoff')

14 right wing

CLOTHING

The players of each team wear matching shirts and shorts, and these must be different enough from those of the opposition to tell them apart. Shirts are usually numbered, with the number indicating the position of the wearer.

Players should be smart in appearance. A smart team is not necessarily a good team, but a good team is invariably of smart appearance. Players may also wear:

- IRB-approved supports made of elasticated, washable materials

- shoulder pads made of soft and thin material, to cover the shoulder and collarbone only

- ankle supports, shinguards, mouth-guards/gumshields

- headgear made of soft, thin material

- items that are worn must bear the authorised mark of the IRB. The referee can order a player to remove any equipment that is unauthorised.

HALF- AND FULL TIME

Referees can only blow their whistle for half-time or the end of the game when the ball has become 'dead'. If a try has been scored, or a penalty kick, free kick, scrum or line-out has been awarded, the referee must allow play to continue until the ball becomes dead again, before blowing for half-time or the end of the game.

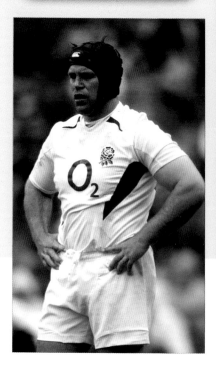

Rugby players are allowed to wear IRB-approved protective equipment. Many forwards choose to wear a headguard or 'scrum cap' like this one.

FOOTWEAR

Players should take great care of their boots, cleaning them thoroughly and keeping the leather in good condition. Manufacturers have to make sure their studs fit IRB regulations. Studs should always be securely fastened. Long studs are more useful than short ones on soft grounds, but they must not be more than 1.8cm in length. Wearing a single stud at the toe of the boot is prohibited.

DURATION OF PLAY

In international matches the game lasts for two periods of 40 minutes each. In other matches the duration of the game is agreed on by the teams, up to a maximum of two periods of 40 minutes each.

Play is divided into two halves, with a maximum half-time break of 10 minutes. At half-time the teams change ends.

Players must not wear any equipment that is likely to cause injury to other players, such as buckles, clips, rings, zips or rigid materials.

A typical pair of rugby boots.

START OF PLAY

Top-level rugby teams spend a lot of time practising the start of play. Mistakes by the team receiving the ball can give a big advantage to the opposition, so they must receive and protect the ball to keep possession. By the same token, the kicking team can gain a big advantage by winning the ball back on its own kick-off.

CHOICE OF END

Before the game starts the home captain tosses a coin, and the visiting captain calls. The winner's team can either:

(a) kick off – the other captain then gets to choose ends, or

(b) choose which end they will play from – the other team then kicks off.

After the half-time interval, the team that didn't start the first half is the one that kicks off.

KICK-OFF

At the start and after half-time, the teams line up in their respective halves of the field (see diagram below). The game begins with a drop kick, taken by any player of the team awarded the kick-off. The ball is kicked from the centre of the halfway line, and must be kicked forwards in the direction of the opponents' 10m line. All players of the kicker's team must stay behind the halfway line until the ball has been kicked.

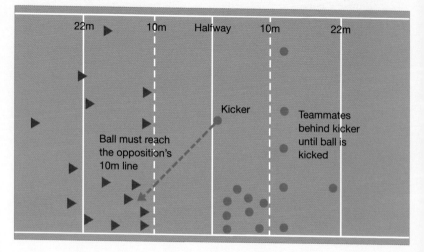

The ball must reach the opponents' 10m line unless an opponent plays it first. If not, and subject to advantage (see page 33), the opposition can choose either another kick-off or a scrum at the centre of the pitch. The team receiving the kick-off must be behind, and remain behind, its 10m line until the ball is kicked, otherwise the kick is taken again.

Straight into touch

If the ball goes straight into touch without touching the ground, the team receiving the kick-off has three choices:

1) they can accept the kick and take a line-out, either at the halfway line or from where the ball went out of play, if that is nearer the kicker's goal line

2) they can have the kick taken again

3) they can take a scrum at the centre spot.

Into in-goal area

If the ball goes into in-goal, the receiving team has three choices:

1) play on

2) ground the ball immediately and take a scrum at the centre spot

3) have the kick taken again.

If the ball goes over the dead-ball line or into touch-in-goal, the receiving team can choose a scrum at the centre or another kick.

> **After a score, the game restarts with a drop kick taken at the centre spot. All the other conditions listed above apply to this kick too.**

Andrew Mehrtens of New Zealand receiving a kick. This is a specialist job, which teams practise again and again, in top-class rugby.

OPEN PLAY

For much of the match, the ball is in 'open play', being passed or kicked between teammates or the two teams. Players with the ball should try either to find space for themselves to run forwards with the ball, or to get the ball to another player with attacking space.

HANDLING

The ball can be passed, thrown or knocked from one player to another in any direction except forwards.

Forward pass

If a player unintentionally throws a forward pass to one of his own team, the referee awards a scrum, with the put-in to the other team, at the place where the infringement occurred.

Knock-on

A knock-on occurs when:

- a player loses possession of the ball, and the ball goes forwards

- the ball hits a player on the hand or arm and goes forwards to touch the ground or another player

- a player fails to catch the ball before it touches the ground (or another player) and the ball bounces up and off their hand or arm.

When a knock-on was accidental, the opposition takes a scrum from where the knock-on occurred. If it was intentional, the opposition gets a penalty kick.

> A knock-on does not occur when the ball travels forwards from the hands or arms of a player who is blocking a kick, as long as he is not trying to catch the ball.

TACKLING

Players are tackled if they are on their feet and have the ball, and are then held by one or more opponents and 'brought to the ground'. If the ball touches the ground, that also makes it a tackle.

Releasing the ball

A tackled player must pass or release the ball at once. Both player and tackler must try to get away from the ball immediately. Players who have been tackled must get to their feet before playing on.

NOT TACKLED

A player is *not* tackled by being:

- lifted off both feet by an opponent
- knocked or thrown over without being held, even if the ball touches the ground.

The player can then pass or release the ball or get up and continue his run.

Falling on the ball

Players are not allowed deliberately to fall on or over a player lying on the ground with the ball in his possession or close to him, or to fall on or over the ball as it comes out of a scrum or ruck.

BROUGHT TO THE GROUND

Ball carriers have been 'brought to the ground' when they:

- have one or both knees on the ground
- are sitting on the ground
- are on top of another player who is on the ground.

Josh Lewsey slides across the line, grounding the ball. If a player who has been tackled slides into the opposition's in-goal area and grounds the ball, it's a try.

KICKING

Kicking provides an alternative to running with or passing the ball. Attacking kicks must be made with the purpose of keeping possession of the ball once it has landed. Defensive kicks tend to put the ball into touch, giving the chance to win the ball back from the resulting line-out.

DROP KICK

To drop kick, players drop the ball and let it fall to the ground before kicking it as it rebounds. A drop kick is used to:

- start the game
- restart after a score
- restart the game at the 22m line after a try, or after the ball has gone into touch-in-goal or over the dead-ball line
- kick at goal after a try has been scored
- score a goal during play.

PLACE KICK

For a place kick the ball is kicked from on the ground, or from a small pile of sand or sawdust, or from an approved kicking tee. It is used to kick at goal after a try has been scored, in which case the kick is taken from a spot opposite where the try was scored and parallel to the touchline. Place kicks are also used for penalty goals.

PUNT

To punt, the player drops the ball and kicks it into the air before it touches the ground. This kick is useful for finding touch or gaining ground, but a goal cannot be scored from it.

The ball is punted with an extended foot, off the laces of the boot. An expert can add a spin to the ball that gives the kick extra length and accuracy, which is called a 'screw kick'. The spin is added by dropping the ball at an angle across the line of the kicking foot.

GRUBBER KICK

A grubber kick is similar to a drop kick, but the ball bounces along the ground rather than rising into the air. The grubber kick is useful for driving the ball between opponents who are near the kicker, or for finding touch when the kicker is outside the 22m area.

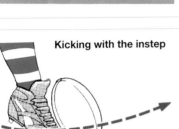
Kicking with the toe

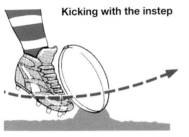
Kicking with the instep

TIME LIMITS

When taking a conversion kick or a penalty kick at goal, the kick must be taken within 4 minutes from the time the kicker indicated an intention to kick.

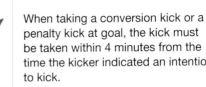
The two most popular kicking placements.

Here, Gavin Henson of Wales strikes a long-distance penalty goal against England.

FREE KICK

Free kicks are awarded for a 'fair catch' and for specific infringements of the rules. Any player can take free kicks awarded for infringements. They must be taken at or behind the place where the free kick was won, on a line parallel to the touchline, and at least 5m from the goal line. A team can choose to take a scrum instead of a free kick.

- Teams cannot score goals from free kicks, and cannot score drop goals until the ball has next become dead or an opponent has played it or tackled the ball carrier.

- The kicker can kick the ball in any direction. Punts and drop kicks are allowed when kicking for touch.

- Players in the kicker's team must be behind the ball until it is kicked.

FAIR CATCH

A fair catch results in a free kick to the catcher. You must catch the ball cleanly from an opponent's kick (except a kick-off) and call 'Mark!' while making the catch. The catcher takes the free kick: if this is not possible within a minute, the team must take a scrum instead.

Philip Murray of Canada takes a fair catch in the air. Players with their feet off the ground may not be tackled, so this is a good way to take catches.

Defending free kicks

Before a free kick, the defending team must wait behind an imaginary line across the field 10m away from the kicker. As soon as the kicker begins, the defenders can run forwards. If the kick is charged down, play continues. Defenders gain a scrum if:

- they prevent the kick, by tackling the kicker, for example

- there is an infringement of the law by the kicker's team.

If there is a free-kick infringement by the defending team, the referee awards a second free kick 10m ahead of the first mark.

Quick free kick

A player can take a quick free kick without waiting for his teammates to get behind the ball, but these players must continue to run back until they are either behind the ball or the player carrying the ball has run past them.

When the quick free kick is taken, the opposing players within 10m of the ball must carry on retreating until they are behind the imaginary 10m line, or until one of their own team, who was behind this line, has run in front of them.

Charlie Hodgson of England barely gets his kick away without it being charged down.

PENALTY KICK

A penalty kick can be taken using a drop kick, a place kick, a tap or a punt. It is taken at the mark or at any point directly behind the mark where the infringement occurred, but not within 5m of the opponents' goal line. A team can choose to take a scrum instead of a penalty kick. Penalty kick outcomes:

- score a goal from a drop kick or place kick

- gain ground by kicking for touch from a punt or drop kick

- gain ground kicking forwards for the kicker's team to follow up if onside.

When the penalty kick is taken (see graphic opposite), the following rules must be observed:

- all the kicker's team-mates must be behind the ball when it is kicked. If a player is in front of the ball, a scrum is formed at the original position. (One player can hold the ball in position for a place kick.)

- players of the defending team must retire without delay behind an imaginary straight line 10m away from the ball, or to their own goal line, whichever is nearer

- for a kick at goal, defenders must stand still with their hands by their sides until the ball has been kicked.

PENALTIES WIN MATCHES

The points scored from penalty kicks often win matches, which is why it is important not to concede penalties – and to have a good penalty kicker in your team.

One of the most accurate penalty kickers ever, the England fly half Jonny Wilkinson.

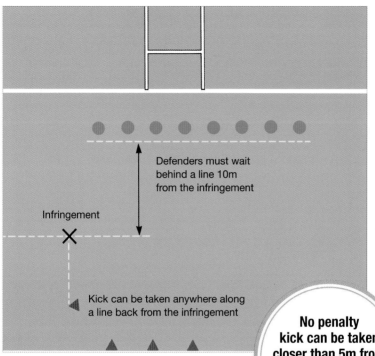

Defenders must wait behind a line 10m from the infringement

Infringement

Kick can be taken anywhere along a line back from the infringement

No penalty kick can be taken closer than 5m from the opponents' goal line.

For an infringement by the opposing team, the kicker's team is given another kick 10m in front of the mark or 5m from the goal line, whichever is the nearer, on a line through the mark parallel to the touchline.

QUICK PENALTY KICK ('TAP PENALTY KICK')

A player can take a quick penalty kick without waiting for his team mates to get behind the ball, but these players must continue to retire until they are onside (behind the ball). Any defenders within 10m of the ball must retire and continue to do so until they are behind the imaginary 10m line, or until one of their own team who was behind this imaginary line has run in front of them.

DEAD BALL

The dead ball gives the players an opportunity for a brief rest. They also get a chance to talk about their tactics, how the game is going, and changes they could make. Referees often use dead-ball breaks to give players instructions about how they are applying the laws of the game.

The ball is 'dead' when it is out of play. This occurs:

- when the ball has gone out of the playing area, or 'out of play', by:
  a) touching or going over the touchline, after which the game is restarted with a line-out (see page 22);
  b) going into the in-goal area and being touched down by a defender;
  c) going over the dead-ball line. In this case, if the attacking team last touched the ball, the game is restarted with a drop kick by the defenders at the 22m line. If a player in the defending team last touched the ball, the game is restarted with a 5m scrum to the attacking side

- when the referee blows his whistle for an infringement

- when a conversion kick after a try has been taken.

TOUCH

The ball is in touch when:

- it touches the ground on or over the touchline, or a person or object on or beyond it (the touchline itself being out of play)

- a player carrying it steps on or touches the touchline, or the ground outside it.

If a player deliberately throws the ball out of play, the referee awards a penalty kick to the opposing team.

The ball is *not* in touch when:

- a player standing in touch kicks a ball which has not touched or crossed the touchline and is in the field of play

- it is blown out of the field of play and back in again without touching the ground.

> **A player is not allowed to throw the ball into touch (or touch-in-goal) deliberately. The punishment is a penalty kick to the opposition.**

TOUCH-IN-GOAL

Touch-in-goal occurs when the ball or player carrying it touches a corner post or a touch-in-goal line, or the ground, or a person or object on or beyond it. The flag itself is not regarded as part of the corner post.

Unfortunately for Munster's John O'Neill, his foot has touched the line before he can ground the ball. He gives the opposition a line-out, rather than scoring a try.

LINE-OUTS

The purpose of the line-out is to bring the ball back into play after it has gone into touch. Possession is not as predictable as at a scrum: there is more chance of winning a line-out against the throw-in than there is in a scrum.

THROW-IN LOCATIONS

When the ball or a player carrying it goes into touch, a throw-in is given to the opposing team. This can be taken as a quick throw-in or as a formed line-out. The place at which it must be thrown in is as follows:

- from penalty kicks, kicks within the kicker's 22m line, and all occasions except those below – at the place where the ball went into touch

- directly into touch after being kicked other than as stated above, or if the kicker got the ball outside the 22m line and retreated behind that line before kicking – opposite the place from which the ball was kicked, or at the place where it went into touch if that is nearer the kicker's goal line

- for a quick throw-in – from between where the ball went into touch and the thrower's goal line.

> If the ball is kicked directly into touch from a penalty kick, the kicking team throws in the ball.

QUICK THROW-INS

A quick throw-in can be taken when:

- the ball that went into touch is used
- the ball has been handled only by the thrower
- the ball is thrown in correctly.

Players' positions for the line-out.

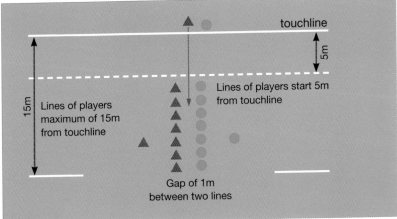

touchline

5m

Lines of players start 5m from touchline

15m Lines of players maximum of 15m from touchline

Gap of 1m between two lines

LINE-OUT

Line-outs contain at least two players from each team. The team throwing in decides how many players will line up. The opposition can have fewer, but not more. They line up in single parallel lines at right angles to the touchline.

- The player taking the throw-in must not step into the field of play. The ball must be thrown in straight between the two lines of players, without feint, and must travel at least 5m before it touches the ground or is caught. If the throw-in is taken incorrectly, the opposition can either take a second throw-in or a scrum 15m from the touchline.

- Players jumping for the ball must not be lifted, but can be supported above the waist after jumping.

- Pushing, charging or interfering with an opponent in the line-out is prohibited unless the opponent has the ball in their possession and feet on the ground, when they can be tackled.

NOT IN THE LINE-OUT

Players further than 15m away from the touchline when the line-out begins are not in the line-out. A player in the line-out can, however, move beyond the 15m line to catch a long throw-in, but only after the ball has left the thrower's hands.

SCRUM, RUCK AND MAUL

The scrummage gets the ball back into play after a stoppage. It is a physically challenging and demanding part of the game. The team throwing in the ball almost always keeps possession; a powerful pack can often tie in defending flank forwards from the opposition before releasing the ball.

SCRUMS

Scrums must always be at least 5m in from the touchline. A scrum can only be formed in the field of play: for infringements in the in-goal area, the scrum is formed 5m from the goal line.

Eight players from each team form the scrum, and no extra players can join it when it is taking place. All eight players must remain bound in the scrum until it ends. They get into formation, then the ball is 'put in' on the ground between them.

Front rows

There must be three players – no more, no less – bound together in the front row. Before the front rows close together, at the mark indicated by the referee, the opposing players must be standing less than an arm's length apart. The ball must be in the scrum half's hands, ready to be put in.

The front rows crouch, so that when they close together each player's shoulders are no lower than their hips. They should come together when the referee calls, 'Engage'. This call is not an order but an indication that the front rows may come together when ready.

The front rows interlock so that no player's head is next to the head of a teammate. Each lock must bind with the prop immediately in front of him. All other players in the scrum must bind with at least one arm and hand around the body of one of the locks.

Formations

There are two basic scrum formations that are adopted by teams: the 3–2–3 and 3–4–1 formations, along with variations such as the 3–3–2 (see diagrams opposite). The 3–4–1 formation is more popular.

Scrum engagement

The referee must call the scrum engagement using the following sequence of verbal commands: 'crouch – hold – engage'. At Under-19 level, the sequence is 'crouch – hold – touch – engage'.

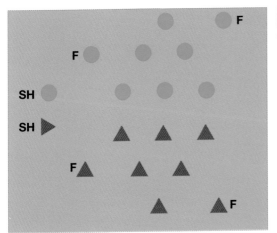

This 3–3–2 allows the flank forwards to link with the half backs more easily.

SH = Scrum half
F = Flank forward

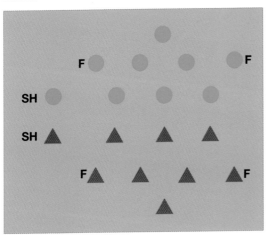

This diagram shows the most popular scrum formation, the 3–4–1.

SH = Scrum half
F = Flank forward

3–4–1 ADVANTAGES

Advantages of the 3–4–1 formation:

- it is a stronger pushing unit, with the flankers fully contributing to the shove
- the ball can be heeled more quickly from the scrum
- when defending, the flankers are nearer to the opposition half backs.

Throwing in the ball

The player throwing in the ball (usually the scrum half) has to:

- stand 1m from the mark on the middle line between the two front rows

- put in the ball with both hands, from a level midway between his knee and ankle, in a single forward movement

- pitch the ball on the ground immediately beyond the nearest player.

Until the ball has left the hands of the player putting it in, no player in either front row may raise either foot from the ground or advance it beyond the line of the feet of his front row. The feet of the nearest players must be far enough back to leave clear the 'tunnel' along which the ball is put in. Once the ball has left the scrum half's hands and is fairly in the scrum, it may be played.

During the scrum

While the ball is in the scrum a player in the front row must not:

- raise both feet off the ground at the same time

- deliberately adopt any position or take any action – for example twisting or lowering the body or pulling on an opponent's clothing – which is likely to cause the scrum to collapse

- deliberately lift an opponent off their feet or force them upwards out of the scrum

- deliberately kick the ball out of the tunnel in the direction from which it was put in.

Front-row play

Front-row players should always try to keep the same basic body position while scrummaging:

- head up: chin off chest, look through the eyebrows

- feet, hips and shoulders should all be squared up

- knees and hips should be bent outwards, with the weight on the balls of the feet

- feet should be planted parallel to the sidelines

- keep the back straight

- the shoulders should be above the hips at all times.

Competing in the air to win the ball.

REFEREEING SCRUMS

- The referee must be strict in penalising deliberate collapsing of the scrum or lifting an opponent off their feet. Either of these acts can result in serious injury.
- If the ball comes out of the scrum at either end of the tunnel, the referee should order it to be put in again. The referee can even award a free kick for wilfully kicking out.

After the scrum half has put the ball in, the hooker heels it back through the scrum. By the time it has come out of the back, the scrum half has come round to direct the next phase of play.

RUCKS

Rucks can only take place on the field of play, and are formed by one or more players. The players stay on their feet, closing round the ball on the ground between them.

When the ball in a ruck becomes unplayable, a scrum is formed. In most cases the team that was moving forward will put the ball in.

MAULS

Mauls can also take place only on the field of play, and are formed by one or more players from each team (at least three in total). The players stay on their feet and close round a player who is carrying the ball. Mauls end when the ball touches the ground, the ball or a player carrying it emerges from the maul, or a scrum is ordered.

When the ball becomes unplayable in a maul, a scrum is formed.

- If the maul is around a player who caught the ball from a kick other than a kick-off or drop-out, and who is immediately held by opponents so that the ball becomes unplayable, the catcher's team put the ball into the scrum.

- In most other cases when the ball becomes unplayable in a maul, the team not in possession before the maul was formed will put the ball in.

SCRUM AND RUCK INFRINGEMENTS

In either a scrum or a ruck:

- players must not return the ball to the scrum or ruck after it has come out, by hand or by foot

- players lying on the ground must not interfere with the ball and must do their best to roll away from the ball

- players must not handle the ball, pick it up with their hands and legs, or intentionally fall or kneel on it, unless the scrum or ruck has moved into either in-goal area.

In a scrum:

- players must not add themselves to the front row to make more than three players in that row

- the player putting in the ball and his opposite number must not kick the ball while it is in the scrum, nor take any action while the ball is in the scrum to convey to the opponents that the ball is out.

It is illegal to collapse a ruck, maul or scrum.

RUCK OR MAUL

Main differences between ruck and maul:

- the position of the ball: ruck – ball on ground; maul – ball carried
- a ruck may have only two players; at least three are needed to form a maul.

 In rucks and mauls, the head and shoulders of all players involved must be no lower than their hips.

Referees and players must work together to ensure that scrums are safe.

SCORING

As in many sports, the team scoring the most points in rugby union wins the match. Points can be scored by any player in the team, and come in the form of a try, conversion, dropped goal or penalty goal. In a tight match, any one of these can easily win the game.

- A try scores five points.
- A goal converted from a try scores two points.
- A goal from a penalty kick or a drop kick scores three points.

The team with the higher number of points wins the match.

TRY

A try is scored if an onside attacking player 'grounds' the ball in his opponents' in-goal. Tries can also be scored if:

- a scrum or ruck pushes over the defenders' goal line and the attackers ground the ball
- a player is stopped from scoring a try by the opposition's unfair play or unlawful interference – in which case the referee should award a penalty try, between the posts.

The goal line is itself within the in-goal area, so a player may score by grounding the ball on the goal line.

Grounding the ball

The ball can be grounded in three ways:

- bringing the ball into contact with the ground while holding it in your hands or arms
- placing your hand(s) or arm(s) on a ball on the ground and exerting downward pressure on it
- falling on a ball on the ground so that it is anywhere under the front of your body, from waist to neck inclusive.

GROUNDING

The purpose of grounding the ball for a defending player is to get out of a dangerous situation and cause a scrum or drop-out. The aim for an attacking player is to score a try.

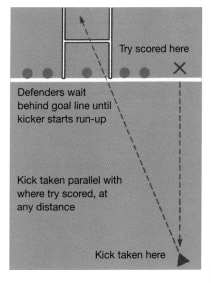

Try scored here

Defenders wait
behind goal line until
kicker starts run-up

Kick taken parallel with
where try scored, at
any distance

Kick taken here

Converting a try.

Brian O'Driscoll of Ireland grounds the
ball to score a try during a Six Nations
Championship match.

GOAL

Goals are scored by:

- converting a try (worth two points)
- a penalty kick (three points)
- a drop kick during play (three points).

Goals are still allowed if the ball passes over the crossbar but is blown back by the wind, or the ball hits the crossbar or goalposts and then goes through.

Goal from penalty kick

Penalty kicks must be taken where the offence occurred or on a line directly behind it. They can be a place kick or a drop kick.

Defenders must retire without delay either 10m from the penalty or to their goal line, whichever is nearer. They must stand still there, with their hands by their sides, until the ball has been kicked. Attackers stay behind the ball while the kick is taken.

Goal from drop kick

A player can drop kick the ball over the opponents' crossbar at any time, scoring three points.

OFFICIALS

The referee and his or her two touch judges are responsible for the smooth running of the game. They must have a complete knowledge of the rules of the game, be able to keep a cool head under presssure, and must be excellent communicators.

REFEREE

The referee applies the laws of the game, and during the match is the only judge of fact and law – all players must accept the referee's decisions without question. The referee also keeps the score and is the timekeeper.

The referee must order off a player who has already been cautioned for obstruction, foul play, misconduct or repeated infringement of the laws, and who repeats the offence. Players sent off must be reported to the organisation under whose jurisdiction the game is being played.

If the referee decides or is advised by a medically trained person that a player is so injured that it would be harmful to continue playing, the referee must ask the player to leave the field. Players who have left the field with an open or bleeding wound may be temporarily replaced until the wound has been dressed.

When referees have made a decision they cannot alter it except:

- when a touch judge has raised a flag to show that the ball has gone out of play

- in certain important matches such as internationals, where

qualified referees are appointed as touch judges, they can indicate to the referee that incidents of foul play or misconduct have occurred by pointing their flag towards the centre field.

IN THE REFEREE'S POCKET:

- a whistle, blown to stop play

- a watch to keep time

- a card and pencil to keep score

- yellow and red cards for disciplining players

- a coin the two captains toss for choice of end.

The referee should keep up with the play, be neutral yet consistent at all times, and limit stoppages to a minimum.

ADVANTAGE LAW

Referees should not whistle for an infringement during play if a stoppage would deprive the non-offending team of an advantage and perhaps the opportunity to score. Play should be allowed to continue. The only exceptions are:

- if a team gains an advantage when the ball or a player carrying it touches the referee

- when the ball emerges from either end of the tunnel at a scrum without having been played.

The referee (on the right) speaking with one of his touch judges.

TOUCH JUDGES

Touch judges hold up their flag to show when and where the ball, or the player carrying it, went into touch or touch-in-goal. They indicate where and by which team the ball should be brought back into play. They lower their flag when the ball has been thrown in properly. The flag stays raised if:

- the ball is thrown in by a player of the team not entitled to do so

- the player throwing in the ball puts any part of either foot into the field of play

- at a quick throw-in, the ball that went into touch is replaced by another or is handled by anyone other than the thrower.

In these cases the opposing team can choose to throw in the ball or take a scrum.

Touch judges also assist the referee by standing behind a goalpost for a kick on goal. If the ball goes over the crossbar they raise their flags.

Touch judge's signals.

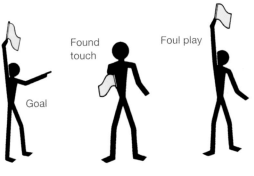

Goal

Found touch

Foul play

OFFENCES

If the referee spots an offence, the team committing the offence will be penalised. Offences can occur at every phase of play; serious offences may result in the perpetrator being shown either the yellow card ('sin-binned') or the red card (permanently sent off).

OFFSIDE IN OPEN PLAY

In general play, players are offside if they are in front of a teammate who has the ball, or in front of the teammate who last played the ball. If players are offside, they are temporarily out of the game. They cannot:

- play the ball or obstruct an opponent

- move towards the opponents waiting to play the ball or the place where the ball pitches, before being played onside

- offside players have to retire without delay and without interference when they are within 10m of an opponent waiting for the ball or of the place where the ball pitches

Failure to do this is punished with a penalty kick to the opponents at the place where the offence occurred, or a scrum at the place where the ball was last played before it occurred. The non-offending team has the option of either award.

OFFSIDE EXCEPTIONS

Exceptions to 'offside in open play':

- moving in front of the kicker at the kick-off, a drop-out, a penalty kick or a free kick (other than at a quick penalty or at a quick free kick), results in a scrum to the opposition, where the kick was taken

- if offside players cannot avoid being touched by the ball or a teammate carrying it, they are 'accidentally offside'. If their team gains no advantage, play continues; if the team does gain advantage, a scrum is awarded to the opposing team.

OFFSIDE AT THE SCRUM

At the scrum, the offside line for the scrum half runs through the ball. For all the other players not in the scrum, the offside line is an imaginary line drawn through the hindmost foot of the last player in the scrum. Being offside at the scrum is punished with a penalty kick.

OFFSIDE AT RUCK AND MAUL

The rules for being offside at a ruck or maul are the same. Players are offside at a ruck or maul if they:

• join the ruck or maul from the opposition's side

• join the ruck or maul in front of the hindmost player of their own team in the ruck or maul

• do not join the ruck or maul but fail to retire behind the offside line without delay

• leave the ruck or maul and do not immediately retire behind the offside line

• advance beyond the offside line with either foot and do not join the ruck or maul.

The penalty is a penalty kick at the place of infringement.

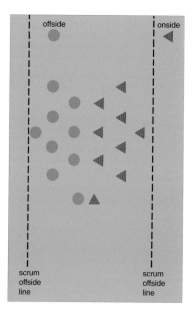

offside   onside

scrum offside line   scrum offside line

The dotted lines show offside and onside positions at the scrum for everyone except the scrum half and the players in the scrum.

The referee awards a penalty for offside at the scrum.

OFFSIDE AT THE LINE-OUT

Players in the line-out are offside if they:

- advance beyond the line of the throw before the ball has touched a player or the ground (unless they do so while jumping for the ball)

- advance in front of the ball after the ball has touched a player or the ground, unless tackling or attempting to tackle an opponent.

Players not taking part in the line-out must stand at least 10m behind the line of touch (the line along which the throw will travel).

▼ **A** kicks the ball forwards, which means **B** is offside. **B** must start to retreat. **X** catches the ball – once **X** has run 5m, **B** becomes onside again, and can rejoin play.

BEING PLAYED ONSIDE

Players who are offside in open play can be played onside, unless they are within 10m of or advancing towards an opponent who is waiting to receive the ball, or of the place where the ball pitches. Offside players are played onside when:

- the opponent in possession of the ball has run 5m

- an opponent has kicked or passed the ball

The penalty for offside at the line-out is awarded at least 15m in from the touchline.

- an opponent intentionally touches the ball, but does not catch it or gather it

- a player of their own team in possession of the ball has run in front of them – provided the offside player is retiring to the imaginary 10m line and is not advancing towards the opponents when they are put onside

- a player of their own team who is behind them kicks the ball

and then runs in front. The kicker and any other onside player can put the player onside. The onside player must be in the field of play or the in-goal, although he can follow up in touch or in touch-in-goal and return to the field of play or in-goal to put the player onside.

- running behind the player of their own team kicking or carrying the ball.

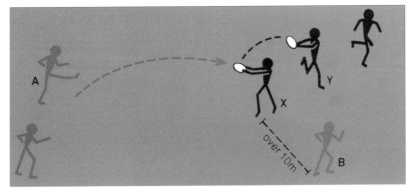

B is offside when **A** kicks the ball. As soon as **X** passes the ball to **Y**, **B** becomes onside again, and can rejoin the game.

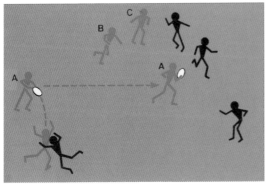

When **A** gets the ball, **B** and **C** are both offside. However, as **A** runs past them with the ball in his hands, they become onside.

BALL TOUCHING REFEREE

- If the ball, or a player carrying it, touches the referee in the field of play, play continues if the referee considers that neither team has gained an advantage. Otherwise a scrum is taken at that spot.

- If the ball, or a player carrying it, touches the referee in the player's in-goal, play continues unless the referee considers that that player's team has gained an advantage, in which case a touchdown is awarded at the spot.

- If the ball or a player carrying the ball in their opponents' in-goal touches the referee, play continues unless the referee considers that that player's team has gained an advantage, in which case a try is awarded at that spot.

- If an attacking player carrying the ball bumps into the referee and this stops a defender from getting to him, any try scored is given at that spot.

BALL TOUCHES REFEREE

If the ball, while in play in in-goal (at either end) and not held by a player, touches the referee or a touch judge:

- a touchdown is awarded if it would otherwise have been obtained, or the ball would have gone dead
- a try is awarded if it would otherwise have been obtained.

Martin Johnson of Leicester Tigers pays close attention to a stern lecture from the referee.

OBSTRUCTION

Obstruction occurs when:

- players running for the ball charge an opponent (except shoulder to shoulder) also running for the ball

- players with the ball after it has come out from a ruck, scrum or line-out attempt to force their way through their own forwards

- offside players 'shield' a member of their own team carrying the ball from an opponent

- players on the outside of the scrum move outwards and thereby prevent an opponent getting round the scrum.

For any of these offences, a penalty kick is awarded at the place of infringement.

MISCONDUCT AND DANGEROUS PLAY

Foul play is prohibited. Players must not:

- hack, trip or strike an opponent

- tackle early, late or dangerously

- charge or obstruct an opponent who has just kicked the ball

- hold, push, charge, obstruct or grasp an opponent not in possession of the ball, except in a scrum, ruck or maul

- cause a scrum, ruck or maul to collapse

- commit any form of misconduct.

If they do, the referee awards a penalty kick, generally at the place of infringement. Any offending players are cautioned, and may be ordered off the field.

A player being yellow-carded or 'sin-binned' – sent from the pitch for 10 minutes of playing time.

VARIATIONS OF RUGBY UNION

Rugby union is not only played using the full 15-a-side laws, which would be too difficult and dangerous for younger players. There are also versions of rugby's laws for children as young as Under-7s. As players get older, the laws change and allow them to develop their skills.

SEVEN-A-SIDE

'Sevens' is played with seven players on each side, on a full-size pitch, and with seven minutes to each half. This allows a lot more space to play in and a lot more space in which to make mistakes!

The winning team in Sevens is often the one that can control the tempo of the game and tire the opposition with superior tactics.

Possession is the key element of Sevens, especially when your side is winning, as the opposition cannot score without the ball.

Sevens tips

- Often, territorial position can be given up in order to keep the ball.

- Drawing the opposition forward as they attempt to win the ball produces even larger gaps for the attack to exploit.

- Teammates must support the ball carrier at all times, but especially if a quick break through the defence is made.

SEVEN-A-SIDE RULES

The laws for Seven-a-side are written by the International Rugby Board (IRB) and can be found at the end of the *Laws of the Game* book or on the IRB's website: www.irb.com.

THE RUGBY CONTINUUM

The Rugby Football Union (RFU) has devised a series of modified games, called together the Rugby Continuum. They allow mixed teams of girls and boys between the ages of 6 and 11 to learn the concepts of rugby in safe, progressive steps, ready for full 15-a-side rugby at the age of 12. The Rugby Continuum is split into six age grades, from Under-7 to Under-12, each with its own specified rules appropriate to the physical and mental skills of the young players. Players are not allowed to play outside of their correct age grade.

All clubs should have a copy of the Rugby Continuum or the 'Tag to Twickenham' coaching cards, which are also on the RFU's website: www.community-rugby.com. The game of rugby is evolving all the time, and so must the rules of the Rugby Continuum. To ensure the safety of young players, everyone involved with these age grades must check the rules to ensure the correct version of the game for a given age level is being played. They should also be properly trained by attending an RFU coaching course, details of which can also be found at www.rfu.com.

PITCH SIZES

Maximum pitch sizes:

Mini Tag Rugby: 60 × 30m plus 2m in-goal area

Touch Rugby: 40 × 30m plus 5m in-goal area

Mini Contact Rugby: 60 × 35m plus 5m in-goal area

Midi Rugby: 60 × 43m plus 5m in-goal area

Jone Daunivucu of Fiji (one of the world's best Sevens teams) pins back his ears during a match against Australia.

MINI TAG RUGBY

Mini Tag Rugby is a completely non-contact game for teams of five to seven players. The emphasis is on the ball carrier's running, handling and evasion, and the running lines of the support players. There are no tackling, kicking, hand-offs, going to ground, scrums or line-outs.

The object of the game is to score a try (five points) by placing the ball with a downward pressure on or behind the opponents' goal line. Each half is 10 minutes long.

Mini Tag rules

- A size 3 ball should be used.

- For the sake of safety, players must remain on their feet at all times.

- The game is started or restarted by a free pass from the centre of the pitch. The opposition must be 7m back, and must not move forward until the ball is passed. The ball must be passed: the player taking the free pass cannot just run with the ball when the referee calls 'Play'.

- For safety reasons, the receiver of the free pass must not start more than 2m from the start point.

- The ball can only be passed sideways or backwards through the air, not handed to another player. If the ball is handed to another player or passed or knocked forward

(towards the opponents' goal line), a free pass is awarded to the opposition, unless advantage can be played.

- Players wear a belt around their waist, with two tags attached to it by Velcro. A 'tag' is the removal of one of the two tags from the ball carrier's belt. Only the ball carrier can be tagged. Ball carriers can run and dodge taggers, but not fend them off using their hands or the ball, and cannot guard or shield tags in any way.

- The ball cannot be pulled out of the ball carrier's hands at any time.

- When tagged, the ball must be passed to a teammate within three seconds or three strides, but can be passed in the act of stopping. Players are only allowed one step to score a try after being tagged and must stay on their feet.

- Diving to score a try is unsafe and must be penalised.

- After the ball has been passed, the player must go to the tagger, retrieve their tag and place it back on their belt before rejoining play. If the player continues to play without collecting their tag, a free pass is awarded to the non-offending side at the place of infringement.

- When a tag is made, the tagger must stop running, hold the tag above their head and shout, 'tag'. If the ball carrier stops running within 1m of their tagger, the tagger must move back towards their own goal line by at least 1m to allow room for the ball to be passed.

- Once the ball has been passed, the tagger must hand the tag back to the player and cannot rejoin the match until this has been done. If a tagger continues to play with an opponent's tag in their hand, or throws it to the floor, a free pass awarded to the opposition at the place of infringement.

- When a 'tag' is made, all players from the tagger's team must attempt to retire towards their own goal line until they are behind the ball, or they will be offside. If a player in an offside position intercepts, prevents or slows down a pass from the tagged player, a free pass will be awarded to the non-offending side.

Players are allowed to run from an onside position to intercept a floated pass before it reaches the intended receiver.

- When the ball is carried into touch, the game is restarted with a free pass awarded to the opposition on the touch line where the ball went out of play.

- The ball carrier must not deliberately make contact with an opponent but should run at the spaces in between the opposition players.

- If the ball goes to ground, players must not dive to the floor to recover it.

- The only contact allowed between the two teams is the removal of a tag from the belt of the ball carrier. Any other type of contact on the ball carrier, such as shirt pulling, running in front of, barging or forcing the ball carrier into touch, etc., is penalised with a free pass.

UNDER-8 MINI TAG VARIATION

During their time in the Under-7 age grade, players may become so good at passing and catching that few mistakes are made, so there are no natural turnovers of the ball. Very often experienced teams score every time they get possession. Because of this, when players move up to the Under-8 age grade a variation is introduced. The side with the ball is only allowed to be tagged a maximum of six times before scoring a try. At the seventh tag, the referee stops the game and gives the ball to the other side, awarding a free pass at the point at which the tag took place.

Referees amend their calls to add the number of the tag as well, so instead of calling 'Tag – Pass', they call, for example, 'Tag – Pass – Three.' On the sixth tag, referees should call 'Tag – Pass – Six and Last', to help players remember the rule. No hand signals are to be used.

SEVENTH TAG

If the seventh tag happens one step from the try line and the ball is grounded, the try is disallowed. The opposition is given the ball for a free pass 7m out from the goal line, in line with the point the goal line was crossed.

TOUCH RUGBY

Touch Rugby is a non-contact game. The emphasis is on running, handling and evasion, and the running lines of the support players. There are no tackling, kicking, hand-offs, scrums or line-outs. Touch Rugby should be played in a similar way to Mini Tag, but with the following differences:

- there are no tag belts in Touch Rugby; a touch tackle is made by placing two hands on the ball carrier's shorts (below the waist) simultaneously, and the ball carrier must pass the ball as detailed in the rules of Mini Tag Rugby

- players should attempt to stay on their feet at all times; however, any player going to ground after a touch tackle must be allowed to get up before passing the ball. If the player has been deliberately pushed to the ground, the offender must be warned, before play restarts with a free pass

- when the ball is carried into touch, the game restarts with a free pass awarded to the opposition 2m in from touch, parallel to the point where the ball or ball carrier crossed the touchline

- when a touch tackle is made, all players from the tagger's team must try to get back behind the ball, or they will be offside. If a player in an offside position intercepts, prevents or slows down a pass from the touched player to a teammate, a free pass is awarded to the opposition. Players are allowed to run from an onside position to intercept a floated pass before it reaches the intended receiver.

In Touch Rugby you are still not allowed to fend off the opposition with your hands or the ball. Dodging and weaving are allowed, though!

Mini Tag Rugby in full flow. It is easy to see how the game improves running and passing skills.

A Mini Tag Rugby player attempts to evade an opposition defender.

MINI CONTACT RUGBY

Mini Contact Rugby brings in tackles and introduces line-outs and scrums, but there are still no kicking or hand-offs. The game starts with a free pass from the centre spot: the rules are the same as for Mini Tag Rugby (see page 42). The game has two halves, each of fifteen minutes. Teams have nine players: three form the scrum, the rest form the back line. The aim is to score a try (five points).

Scrums

If the ball is passed or knocked forward, a scrum is awarded to the opposition, unless advantage can be played. Scrums are made up of one row of three players from each team, i.e. a prop on either side of the hooker. The referee talks the players through the engagement procedure in the sequence 'Crouch, Touch' (when the props place a hand on their opposite number's arm), 'Pause' and 'Engage'.

Scrums are uncontested at Under-9 and contested at Under-10. In contested scrums, the players may push and strike for the ball when it is put in. The scrum must not be allowed to move more than 1.5m towards either try line or wheel more than 45 degrees.

The back line of the team not throwing the ball into the scrum must remain 7m behind the scrum until the

Mini Contact Rugby for Under-9s is the first time young rugby players experience scrums. At Under-10, the scrums can be contested.

ball emerges or the scrum half places his hands on it. Until this happens, the opposing scrum half must remain directly behind his scrum.

Tackling

- Tacklers must immediately release the tackled player and get up or move away. The tackler must get up before playing the ball.

- Tackled players must immediately pass or release the ball, and get up or move away from the ball. They can put or push the ball on the ground in any direction except forward, providing it is done immediately.

▼ Mini Contact Rugby is the first time players are allowed to make tackles.

- At or near a tackle, other players must play the ball from behind the ball and tackled player, or the tackler closest to their goal line.

- Tackles level with or above the armpit and scrag-type tackles (swinging the player by the shirt) are dangerous play and are penalised.

A size 3 ball should be used for Under-9s; a size 4 for Under-10s.

Mauls

Mauls occur when a player carrying the ball is held by one or more opponents, and one or more of the ball carrier's team mates bind on to the ball carrier. All the players involved are to be on their feet.

- Mauls end successfully when the ball or ball carrier leaves the maul; the ball is on the ground; or is on or over the goal line.

- Mauls end unsuccessfully if the ball becomes unplayable or the maul collapses (not as the result of foul play) and a scrum is awarded.

Rucks

A ruck occurs where one or more players from each team, who are on their feet and in physical contact, close around the ball on the ground. 'Rucking' describes using your feet to try and win or keep possession of the ball, without being guilty of foul play.

- A ruck ends successfully when the ball leaves the ruck, or is on or over the goal line.

- A ruck ends unsuccessfully when the ball becomes unplayable and a scrum is awarded. The throw-in goes to the team that the referee decides was moving forward.

BALL EMERGING

When a maul remains stationary or has stopped moving forward for more than five seconds, but the ball is being moved and the referee can see it, a reasonable time is allowed for the ball to emerge. If it does not emerge within a reasonable time, a scrum is awarded to the team not in possession of the ball when the maul began.

Rucks and mauls are allowed in Mini Contact Rugby.

Line-outs

When the ball or ball carrier goes out of play, a line-out is held where the ball or players crossed the touchline. The opponents of the team who carried or last touched the ball before it went into touch throw the ball in. Line-outs extend from 2 to 7m from the touchline, and are uncontested at Under-9 and contested at Under-10.

> **Quick line-out throw-ins are not allowed in Mini Contact.**

Numbers in the line-out

The line-out contains two players from each team, the player throwing the ball in and an immediate opponent, who must stand within the 2m area. One player from either side stands in a position to receive the ball (i.e. scrum half).

Both the thrower and his or her immediate opponent can join the game as soon as the ball has been touched by one of the players in the line-out. The ball must be thrown into the line-out (i.e. between 2 and 7m), not beyond it.

- Lifting or supporting a line-out jumper is not allowed.

- The offside line for all players not in the line-out is 7m back from the line of touch parallel to the goal line. They must remain behind that offside line until the line-out has ended.

Supporting the person jumping for the ball is not allowed in Mini Contact Rugby, which tends to mean it is less easy for the team throwing in to win the ball.

MIDI RUGBY

Midi Rugby builds and expands on the concepts learned in Mini Contact Rugby. Kicking is allowed, but there are still no 'fly hacking' (kicking a free ball on the floor) or hand-offs. The aim is to score tries (five points) and conversions (two points). The game has two halves of 20 minutes.

There are 12 players in each team in midi: five form the scrum, the other seven form the back line. A size 4 ball is used for Under-11s and Under-12s. The rules for tackling, knock-ons, mauling and rucking are similar to those for Mini Contact Rugby (see pages 47–49). The rules for starting play, scrums and line-outs are different.

Starting play

Play is started with a drop kick from the centre of the pitch.

Scrums

Midi Rugby scrums are made up of five players on each side. Scrums are contested at Under-11 and Under-12. Three players form the front row and two other players bind on to them to form the second row. As with Mini Contact, the front rows from each team bind together approximately half a metre apart; the props touch the upper arm of their opponent, then pause before engaging. The referee talks the players through the engagement procedure in sequence: 'Crouch, Touch, Pause' and 'Engage'.

Line-outs

Line-outs are contested at Under-11 and Under-12. The line-out extends from 2 to 10m from the touchline. It is made up of four players from each team, plus the player throwing the ball in and an immediate opponent, who must stand within the 2m area. One player from either side stands in a position to receive the ball (i.e. scrum half).

The ball has to be thrown into the line-out, not beyond it, and should be caught only by a line-out player. After the throw-in, the thrower and his opposite number can only start playing again once the ball has been touched by a player in the line-out. Lifting or supporting a line-out jumper is not allowed.

The offside line for all players not participating in the line-out is the same as in Mini Contact Rugby (see page 49).

BALL IN SCRUM

The back line of the team not throwing the ball into the scrum must stay behind the back feet of the rearmost players in the scrum until the ball emerges or the scrum half places his hands on it. Until this happens, the opposing scrum half must not move beyond the centre line of the scrum.

Conversions

Conversions of tries are allowed in Midi Rugby: the kick at goal takes place from anywhere in front of the posts. Drop goals are not allowed.

Midi Rugby players cannot be supported by their teammates, so must leap under their own steam. This makes timing their jump well crucial to success.

Quick throw-ins are allowed in Midi Rugby. See page 22 for the rules about when these are allowed.

UNDER-15 RUGBY

At the Under-13 age grade, players switch to a 15-a-side game, the rules for which are contained in the Under-15 law variations. These rules are followed by players in the Under-13, Under-14 and Under-15 age grades, and are variations on the Under-19 laws laid down by the IRB.

The current variations from the Under-19 laws (see below for these) are as follows:

- no supporting in the line-out

- sides with clearly stronger scrummagers will be told by the referee to ensure their opposition are not pushed off their feet. If they do not comply, uncontested scrums must be ordered

- the opposing scrum half cannot follow the ball past the centre line of the scrum.

UNDER-19 VARIATIONS

The Under-19 variations of the game are written by the International Rugby Board (IRB) and can be found at the end of the Laws of the Game book or on the IRB's website: www.irb.com.

Duration

- The game lasts for 35 minutes each half.

Line-outs

- Supporting in the line-out is allowed, but players must not support a jumping teammate below the waist.

Scrums

- Scrums have a maximum of eight players in a 3–4–1 formation, but reduce in number if fewer than 15 players can be fielded, to a minimum of five.

REDUCED SCRUMS

If there are fewer than 15 players available, scrums reduce in number as follows:

- if one player short, 3–4 formation
- if two short, 3–2–1 formation
- if three short, 3–2 formation.

- If a side does not have specifically trained front-row or second-row players, scrums must be uncontested.

- A scrum must not be pushed more than 1.5m or wheeled more than 45 degrees.

- Once the ball is at the back of the scrum it must be played immediately.

LAW VARIATIONS

Rugby's laws are constantly under review to keep pace with the modern game. The RFU's website (see below) should be consulted regularly for any updates.

THE RUGBY FOOTBALL UNION

The Rugby Football Union was established in 1871 and celebrated its 125th anniversary in 1996. For more details on the game of rugby union and for information on publications, videos and recent law changes, contact: The Rugby Football Union, Rugby Road, Twickenham, Middlesex TW1 1DZ. Website: www.rfu.com

A Wales v. Ireland Under-21 match: in this age group, the players are playing the full, adult version of the game.

RUGBY CHRONOLOGY

1820s and 1830s Boys from Rugby School gradually develop and shape the game that will become famous worldwide.

1845 Three boys at Rugby School publish their first set of written rules. These are the first written rules for any form of 'football' and are one of the reasons why Rugby's game flourished while others died out.

1854 Trinity College, Dublin is the first rugby club to be formed in Ireland.

1858 Edinburgh Academicals is the first rugby club to be formed in Scotland.

1872 First match between Oxford and Cambridge Universities. Oxford wins by one goal to nil. This fixture will become known as the 'Varsity' match.

1873 Scottish Rugby Football Union founded.

1874 Two rugby unions formed in Ireland. The Irish Football Union represents players from Munster, Leinster and Connaught. The Northern Football Union of Ireland represents players from Ulster. They agree to select a number of players each for Ireland's international fixtures.

1875 15 February – Ireland's first international fixture, played against England at the Oval, London. England win.

13 December – Oxford and Cambridge are the first to reduce their teams from 20 to 15-a-side.

Two clubs, Hamilton and Villagers, are formed in South Africa. Both claim to be the oldest clubs in that country.

1877 5 February – England and Ireland meet at The Oval, London to contest the first international match played between teams of 15-a-side. England win.

1878 RFU is offered a cup from the disbanded Calcutta Club of India as a trophy for a knock-out club competition. Soccer's FA Cup is proving very popular at the time and they envisage a rugby equivalent. The RFU refuses to accept it for this purpose (since they believe that 'competitiveness' runs against the amateur ethos) but does accept it for use in fixtures against Scotland.

1879 The two Irish unions combine to form the Irish Rugby Football Union.

1880 28 February – England become the first winners of the Calcutta Cup when they defeat Scotland.

1881 19 February – Wales' first international fixture is played, against England. The match is played three weeks before the formation of the Welsh Rugby Union. England win.

1882 First ever overseas tour, when New South Wales travel to New Zealand. The tourists expect to win all of their seven games, but underestimate the strength of the New Zealanders and only win four.

1884 First New Zealand tour, to New South Wales (Australia). The tourists do not play any tests, but win all of their matches.

1885 For the first time, referees are given a whistle and umpires given sticks (later flags).

1886 The International Rugby Football Board (IRFB) is formed by Scotland, Ireland and Wales. England declines to join since they believe they should have greater representation on the board for having a greater number of clubs. They also refuse to accept that the IRFB should be the recognised lawmaker of the game. The IRFB agrees that the member countries will not play England until the RFU agrees to join. Points for scoring adopted by IRFB.

1888 A privately financed team of British players organised by two cricket promoters tours New Zealand and Australia. Although there are rumours that the players have been paid expenses for their clothes, Jack Clowes of Halifax is the only player to admit to it. He is declared a professional by the RFU and banned from playing rugby.

New Zealand Native team tours Great Britain, Australia and New Zealand. On the longest tour ever, they play 107 matches, winning 78, drawing 6 and losing 23. The tour lasts for over a year.

1889 South African RFU founded.

1890 England becomes a member of the IRFB.

1891 South Africa's first international fixture. They lose 4–0 against the touring British Isles team in Port Elizabeth. This was also the first time a British team had toured South Africa. They win all 20 matches of the tour, conceding only one point. They remain the only British Isles side to win every game on a tour.

1892 New Zealand Rugby Football Union founded.

1893 At the RFU's AGM, Yorkshire complain that, although there are more rugby clubs in the North of England than in the South, more Southerners than Northerners populate the RFU Committee. Also, Committee meetings are held in London at times that are not suitable for northern folk to attend.

1895 29 August – At a meeting at the George Hotel, Huddersfield, 20 clubs from Yorkshire, Lancashire and Cheshire decide to resign from the RFU and form the Northern Rugby Football Union (from 1922 it would be known as Rugby League).

Zimbabwe RFU founded (known as Rhodesia RFU until 1980).

1899 Australia's first international fixture. They defeat the touring British Isles side 13–3 at the Sydney Cricket Ground.

The first Irish team tours overseas. They tour Canada, playing 11 games, winning 10 and losing one, but do not play any tests.

Argentinian Rugby Union founded.

1900 Rugby played at the Olympic Games for the first time. Only two countries enter: France defeat Germany 25–16.

1903 New Zealand's first international fixture. They defeat Australia 22–3 at the Sydney Cricket Ground.

1905 The New Zealand 'Originals' tour the British Isles, France and America, playing 35 matches. They win 34 games, losing only one – to Wales.

First Australia tour, to New Zealand. Even with the strongest New Zealand players touring on the other side of the world, the Australians only win three of the seven games they play.

1906 South Africa tour the British Isles and France for the first time. They play 28 games, winning 25, drawing one and losing two.

1908 Australia tour the British Isles for the first time. They play 31 matches, winning 25, drawing one and losing five. The Australian team receives three shillings a day for out-of-pocket expenses and Scotland refuse to play the team, claiming that paying them makes them professionals.

Rugby is played at the Olympic Games for the second time and only two countries enter. Australia defeat Great Britain 32–3.

1910 The Five Nations Championship begins. This is the first year that England, Scotland, Ireland, Wales and France play each other in the same season. Even though the Championship is not formally recognised for many years to come, England are the first champions after winning three and drawing one of their four games.

A British Isles side visits Argentina for the first time. They play six games and win them all.

1913 Fijian Rugby Union founded.

1914 4 August – Nine days after the outbreak of World War I, an RFU circular advises all players to join the armed forces. 133 international players from the British Isles, Australia, New Zealand, South Africa, France and Romania will die during the conflict.

1919 French Rugby Federation founded.

1920 Rugby is played at the Olympics for the third time and only two countries enter. USA defeat France 8–0.

1923 Spanish Rugby Federation founded.

Tongan RFU founded.

1924 USA rugby team tours Britain to 'warm up' for the Olympic Games.
Rugby is played at the Olympics for the last time. Three countries enter and the USA win the gold by defeating the other two nations – Romania and France. After these games, the International Olympic Committee decides to discontinue events such as rugby, which attracted minimal entrants.

Samoan RFU founded.

1925 The New Zealand 'Invincibles' tour the British Isles, France and Canada. They play 32 matches and win them all.

1926 Japanese RFU founded.

1928 Italian Rugby Federation founded.

1929 Italy's first international fixture. They lose 9–0 to Spain.

1930 All future matches are to be played under the laws of the IRFB.

1931 Ten French clubs attempt to break away from the French Federation to form their own union. The Home Unions, concerned about alleged illegal payments to players and foul play in the French game, agree to suspend relations with the French Federation until it can prove that it has control over the game.

Romanian Rugby Federation founded.

1934 Federation Internationale de Rugby Amateur (FIRA) is formed at the instigation of the French. It is designed to organise the game outside of the major rugby-playing nations. The founding members are France, Italy, Germany, Portugal, Sweden, Romania, Catalonia (part of Spain), Holland and Czechoslovakia.

1939 France is invited to rejoin the Five Nations Championship for the following season, but war is declared and international rugby is suspended. 88 international players from the British Isles, New Zealand, Australia, South Africa, France, Germany and Romania are killed during the conflict.

The ban on Rugby League players is temporarily lifted by the RFU. Many play in the eight Services Internationals played between England and Scotland during the war years.

1947 France plays its first Five Nations games since 1931 as the championship restarts after the war.

1949 Australia, New Zealand and South Africa become members of the IRFB. Australian Rugby Union founded.

First France tour, to Argentina. The tourists win all nine games, including the two test matches.

1951 Uruguay Rugby Union founded.

1957 To celebrate the fact that England have won all of their Five Nations games that year, *The Times* newspaper uses the expression 'Grand Slam'. This is possibly the first time the expression is used in this context.

1960 First Scotland tour, to South Africa. This is the first ever short international tour. Even though the tourists lose the test, the tour itself is seen as a success and, in the way in which it is set up and conducted, sets the standard to follow.

1963 First England tour, to New Zealand and Australia. The tourists play three tests in eleven days and lose them all.

1964 First Wales tour, to South Africa. The tourists win the majority of their games but the only test sees them suffer their biggest test defeat in 40 years.

Georgian Rugby Union founded.

1965 Canadian Rugby Union founded.

1975 United States of America Rugby Union founded.

1978 France becomes a member of the IRFB.

1980 First Italy tour, to New Zealand. The tourists win two of the five matches and do not play any tests.

1981 Anti-apartheid demonstrations lead to the disruption of the South African tour of New Zealand. Games are cancelled and, in the final test, a plane drops flour bombs and pamphlets on the pitch while the game is in progress.

1983 Formation of the Women's Rugby Football Union, covering the countries of the British Isles.

1986 New Zealand 'Cavaliers' travel for an illegal and unofficial tour of South Africa. This leads to the players having a ban imposed on them by the NZRFU when they return home. Allegations that they had received payment for playing are never proven.
Canada becomes a member of the IRFB.

1987 First Rugby World Cup tournament is held in Australia and New Zealand. New Zealand defeats France in the final 29–9 at Eden Park, Auckland.
Argentina, Fiji, Italy, Japan, Romania, Tonga, USA and Zimbabwe become members of the IRFB.

1988 Cote d'Ivoire, Spain and Samoa become members of the IRFB.

1989 Uruguay becomes a member of the IRFB.

1990 Namibian Rugby Union founded.
Namibia becomes a member of the IRFB.

1991 Second Rugby World Cup tournament is held in the British Isles and France.
Australia defeats England in the final 12–6.

1992 South Africa plays its first international fixture since 1984, after apartheid policies are repealed. They lose to New Zealand 27–24.
Georgia becomes a member of the IRFB.

1995 Third Rugby World Cup tournament is held in South Africa. South Africa defeats New Zealand in the final 15–12.

26 August – After years of revision to the amateur regulations of the game, the IRFB concludes that the only way to keep control of rugby is to declare the game 'open' – or professional.

1996 The Tri-Nations Tournament involving Australia, New Zealand and South Africa begins. Played on a home-and-away basis, New Zealand win all of their four matches and become the inaugural champions.

1997 White Card and 'sin-bin' introduced by laws committee to discourage the 'professional foul'. These will later become red and yellow cards.

1998 The International Rugby Football Board drops the 'F' to become the IRB.

1999 Scotland is the last winner of the Five Nations Championship.
Fourth Rugby World Cup tournament is held in the British Isles and France. Australia defeats France in the final 35–12.

2000 The Five Nations becomes Six when Italy joins. They win the first game of the new championship, defeating Scotland 34–20.

2002 6 April – France become the first team to win a 'Grand Slam' in the Six Nations Championship.

2003 Fifth Rugby World Cup tournament is held in Australia. England defeat Australia in the final 20–17.

INTERNATIONAL HONOURS

The Rugby World Cup

The driving force behind the creation of a Rugby World Cup competition had been the countries of the Southern Hemisphere. The first finals were jointly held in Australia and New Zealand in 1987 and the rugby landscape changed forever. No longer is the title of 'best team in the world' one of pure speculation.

World Cup Winners		
New Zealand	1	1987
Australia	2	1991, 1999
South Africa	1	1995
England	1	2003

The Tri-Nations

The Southern Hemisphere superpowers (Australia, New Zealand and South Africa) only met occasionally and could only look on in envy at the Five Nations Championship. It was after the third Rugby World Cup, in South Africa in 1995, that the Tri-Nations was born. The impetus behind it was that year's acceptance of professionalism in rugby union, with a big television deal funding the tournament.

Tri-Nations Winners		
New Zealand	6	1996, 1997, 1999, 2002, 2003, 2005
Australia	2	2000, 2001
South Africa	2	1998, 2004

The Six Nations Championship

A series of annual friendly matches between England, Scotland, Ireland, Wales and France was gradually turned into the Five Nations 'competition' by the press, who created tables and awarded points. The competition only gained official status in 1993 with the first presentation of The Five Nations Championship Trophy. Italy was invited to join the competition in 2000.

Five/Six Nations Championship Winners

1910	**England**
1911	Wales
1912	**England and Ireland**
1913	England
1914	**England**
1920	England, Scotland and Wales
1921	**England**
1922	Wales
1923	**England**
1924	England
1925	**Scotland**
1926	Scotland and Ireland
1927	**Scotland and Ireland**
1928	England
1929	**Scotland**
1930	England
1931	**Wales**
1932	England, Wales and Ireland
1933	**Scotland**
1934	England
1935	**Ireland**
1936	Wales
1937	**England**
1938	Scotland
1939	**England, Wales and Ireland**
1947	Wales and England
1948	**Ireland**
1949	Ireland
1950	**Wales**
1951	Ireland
1952	**Wales**
1953	England
1954	**England, France and Wales**
1955	France and Wales
1956	**Wales**
1957	England
1958	**England**
1959	France
1960	**France and England**
1961	France
1962	**France**
1963	England
1964	**Scotland and Wales**
1965	Wales
1966	**Wales**
1967	France
1968	**France**
1969	Wales
1970	**France and Wales**
1971	Wales
1972	*****
1973	Quintuple tie
1974	**Ireland**
1975	Wales
1976	**Wales**
1977	France
1978	**Wales**
1979	Wales
1980	**England**
1981	France
1982	**Ireland**
1983	France and Ireland
1984	**Scotland**
1985	Ireland
1986	**France and Scotland**
1987	France
1988	**Wales and France**
1989	France
1990	**Scotland**
1991	England
1992	**England**
1993	France
1994	**Wales**
1995	England
1996	**England**
1997	France
1998	**France**
1999	Scotland
2000	**England**
2001	England
2002	**France**
2003	England
2004	**France**
2005	Wales

* = season not completed

INDEX